This book belongs to

....

Mum's New Hat and Other stories

How this collection works

This *Biff, Chip and Kipper* collection is one of a series of four books at **Read with Oxford Stage 1**. It is divided into two distinct halves.

The first half focuses on phonics-based reading practice, with phonics activities in *Biff's Fun Phonics* and *Kipper's Rhymes*. The second half contains three stories that use everyday language: *A Good Trick*, *The Pancake* and *Mum's New Hat*. These stories help to broaden your child's wider reading experience. There are also fun activities to enjoy throughout the book.

How to use this book

Find a time to read with your child when they are not too tired and are happy to concentrate for about ten minutes. Reading at this stage should be a shared and enjoyable experience. It is best to choose just one story or phonics activity for each session.

There are tips for each part of the book to help you make the most of the activities and stories. The tips for reading on pages 6 and 28 show you how to introduce your child to the phonics activities.

The tips for reading on pages 50, 62 and 74 explain how you can best approach reading the stories that use a wider vocabulary. At the end of each story you will find four 'Talk about the story' questions. These will help your child to think about what they have read, and to relate the story to their own experiences. The questions are followed by a fun activity.

Enjoy sharing the stories!

Authors and illustrators

Biff's Fun Phonics written by Annemarie Young, illustrated by Nick Schon
Kipper's Rhymes written by Annemarie Young, illustrated by Alex Brychta
A Good Trick written by Roderick Hunt, illustrated by Alex Brychta
The Pancake written by Roderick Hunt, illustrated by Alex Brychta
Mum's New Hat written by Roderick Hunt, illustrated by Alex Brychta

OXFORD
UNIVERSITY PRESS

Great Clarendon Street, Oxford, OX2 6DP, United Kingdom

Oxford University Press is a department of the University
of Oxford. It furthers the University's objective of excellence
in research, scholarship, and education by publishing
worldwide. Oxford is a registered trade mark of Oxford
University Press in the UK and in certain other countries

Mum's New Hat first published in 2006
The Pancake first published in 1999
A Good Trick first published in 1998
Kipper's Rhymes, *Biff's Fun Phonics* first published in 2013
This Edition published in 2018

British Library Cataloguing in Publication Data
Data available

ISBN: 978-0-19-276417-1

10 9 8 7 6 5 4 3

Paper used in the production of this book is a natural, recyclable product
made from wood grown in sustainable forests. The manufacturing process
conforms to the environmental regulations of the country of origin.

Printed in Great Britain by Bell and Bain Ltd, Glasgow

Acknowledgements

Series Editors: Annemarie Young and Kate Ruttle

Contents

OXFORD
UNIVERSITY PRESS

Phonics

Tips for reading *Biff's Fun Phonics*

Children learn best when reading is relaxed and enjoyable.

- Tell your child that they are going to help Biff read and look for things in the pictures.

- Ask your child to read the captions and sentences on the left-hand page. Then ask them to match them to the correct picture on the right-hand page.

- Don't forget that when you talk about letter sounds, say the letter sound clearly, for example, for the sound 'm' as in mug, you say 'mmm' not 'em'. You can listen to the letter sounds at **oxfordowl.co.uk.**

- Give lots of praise as your child reads with you and does the activities.

- Play the game on page 26 to help the muddy pup get to the bath.

Have fun!

How many spiders can you find hidden in the pictures?

This story practises these letter sounds:

    s a t p i n m d
    g o c ck e u r h
    b f l v ff ll ss

For more activities, free eBooks and practical advice to help your child progress with reading visit **oxfordowl.co.uk**

Biff's Fun Phonics

Match the captions to the pictures.

Read the two captions.
Can you match each caption
to its picture?

a cap on a peg

a cup and a mug

Read the two captions.
Can you match each caption
to its picture?

cod in a pan

carrots in a pot

 Read these captions. Can you match the captions to the pictures?

red on the rug

mess on the mat

 Read the sentences. Can you find the rabbit and the pup in the picture?

The rabbit is in the hut.

The pup is in the mud.

Read the sentences. Which
one matches the picture?

Get off the bus.

Get a hug and
a kiss.

dy Fashions

21

 Read the sentences. Which one matches the picture?

A nut on the bag.

Get on top of the rock.

23

 Read the sentences. Can you find the rabbit and the duck in the picture?

The rabbit is at the vet.

The duck is on top.

Muddy maze

Help the muddy pup get to the bath.

Tips for reading *Kipper's Rhymes*

Children learn best when reading is relaxed and enjoyable.

- Tell your child that they are going to help Kipper read some fun rhymes and play 'I spy'.

- Ask your child to read the rhymes on the left-hand page. Then ask them to find the objects in the scene on the right-hand page.

- Once they have done this, ask them to find other rhyming objects in the picture.

- Don't forget that when you talk about letter sounds, say the letter sound clearly, for example, for the sound 'm', you say 'mmm' not 'em'. You can listen to the letter sounds at **oxfordowl.co.uk.**

- Give lots of praise as your child reads with you and does the activities.

- Play the game on page 48 to help Dad find his way home in the fog.

Have fun!

Find the robin hidden in every picture.

This book practises these letter sounds:

s   a   t   p   i   n   m   d   g   o
c   k   ck   e   u   r   h   b   f   l   j
w   ff   ll   ss

 For more activities, free eBooks and practical advice to help your child progress with reading visit **oxfordowl.co.uk**

Kipper's Rhymes

Read the rhyming words and find the objects in the pictures.

Read these rhyming words and
find them in the picture.

A bug in a mug.

A jug on the rug.

What else can you
find in the picture that
rhymes with **mug**?

hug, slug

Read these rhyming words and
find them in the picture.

A wet pet!

A fan and a can.

What other things
can you find in the
picture that rhyme with
pet and **can**?

jet, net, man, pan

33

Read these rhyming words and
find them in the picture.

Less mess, Biff!

Ted is on the bed.

What things can you
find in the picture that
rhyme with **sock**?

clock, rock

Read these rhyming words and
find them in the picture.

Hop to the top.

Bill is on the hill.

What else can you
find in the picture that
rhymes with **top**?

mop, pop

Read these rhyming words and
find them in the picture.

A dog on a log.

Huff and puff!

What else can you
find in the picture that
rhymes with **dog**?

fog, jog, bog

Read these rhyming words and
find them in the picture.

Jack and his backpack.

Mack in a sack.

What else can you
find in the picture that
rhymes with **sack**?

track

41

Read these rhyming words and
find them in the picture.

The hen is in a pen.

The egg is on
a peg.

What else can you
find in the picture that
rhymes with **pen**
and **peg**?

ten, men, leg

Read these rhyming words and
find them in the picture.

A ticket in a pocket.

A rocket in a bucket.

What can you
find in the picture that
rhymes with **duck**?

truck

Read these rhyming words and find them in the picture.

Pat a cat.

A rat sat on a mat.

What else can you find in the picture that rhymes with **cat**?

hat, bat

Maze haze

Help Dad get home in the fog.

Stories for Wider Reading

Tips for reading the stories together

These three stories use simple everyday language. Encourage your child to read as much as they can with you. You can help your child to read any longer words, like 'wind' and 'blew', in the context of the story. Children enjoy re-reading stories and this helps to build their confidence and their vocabulary.

Tips for reading *A Good Trick*

- Talk about the title and look through the pictures so that your child can see what the story is about.

- Read the story to your child, placing your finger under each word as you read.

- Read the story again and encourage your child to join in.

- Give lots of praise as your child reads with you.

- Talk about the story.

- Do the fun activity on page 60.

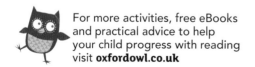

For more activities, free eBooks and practical advice to help your child progress with reading visit **oxfordowl.co.uk**

Have fun!

A Good Trick

A rug,

a sheet,

a big box,

55

a little box,

57

Kipper!

Talk about the story

Spot the difference

Find the five differences in the two pictures.

Tips for reading *The Pancake*

- Talk about the title and look through the pictures so that your child can see what the story is about.
- Read the story to your child, placing your finger under each word as you read.
- Read the story again and encourage your child to join in.
- Give lots of praise as your child reads with you.
- Talk about the story.
- Do the fun activity on page 72.

For more activities, free eBooks and practical advice to help your child progress with reading visit **oxfordowl.co.uk**

Have fun!

The Pancake

The frying pan,

the flour,

the eggs,

the milk,

the butter,

the pancake.

The pancake race!

Talk about the story

What went into the pancake?

Who stirred the pancake mixture?

What did Dad do with the pancake?

What is your favourite pancake filling?

Spot the difference

Find the five differences in the two pictures.

Tips for reading *Mum's New Hat*

- Talk about the title and look through the pictures so that your child can see what the story is about.
- Read the story to your child, placing your finger under each word as you read.
- Read the story again and encourage your child to join in.
- Give lots of praise as your child reads with you.
- Talk about the story.
- Do the fun activity on page 94.

Have fun!

After you have read the story, find the feather hidden in every picture.

This story includes these useful common words:

the   get   my   said

For more activities, free eBooks and practical advice to help your child progress with reading visit **oxfordowl.co.uk**

Mum's New Hat

The wind blew Mum's hat off.

Mum had a new hat.

The wind blew.

It blew Mum's hat off.

"Get my hat," said Mum.

Dad ran.

The wind blew.

Oh no!

"Get that hat," said Dad.

Kipper ran.

The wind blew.

Oh no!

"Get that hat," said Kipper.

Biff ran.

The wind blew.

Oh no!

"Look at my new hat!"
said Mum.

Talk about the story

How did Mum lose her new hat?

Why do you think Biff has a camera?

What funny things happened to Mum's hat?

Have any funny things happened to you on windy days?

A maze

Help Mum get her hat.

Remembering the stories together

Encourage your child to remember and retell the three stories in this book. You could ask questions like these:

- Who are the characters in the story?
- What happens at the beginning of the story?
- What happens next?
- How does the story end?
- What was your favourite part of the story? Why?

Story prompts

When talking to your child about the stories, you could use these more detailed reminders to help them remember the exact sequence of events. Turn the statements below into questions, so that your child can give you the answers. For example, *What are Biff and Chip doing with a sheet? Who's hiding inside?* And so on …

A Good Trick

- Biff and Chip are doing some tricks.
- They use a rug, a sheet, a big box, a little box …
- And who's inside the box? Kipper.

The Pancake

- Dad decides to make pancakes with the children.

- They put in the flour and eggs.

- Then the milk and butter.

- Dad tosses the pancake …

- And Mum wins a pancake race!

Mum's New Hat

- Mum and Dad are going to a wedding, so Mum gets a new hat.

- It's a bit windy and her hat blows away.

- They all chase after it.

- Oh no! Someone runs over Mum's hat with their bike.

- It blows away again, so they keep chasing.

- They find the hat stuck to a freshly painted bench. It's a bit of a mess!

You could now encourage your child to create a 'story map' of each story, drawing and colouring all the key parts of them. This will help them to identify the main elements of the stories and learn to create their own stories.